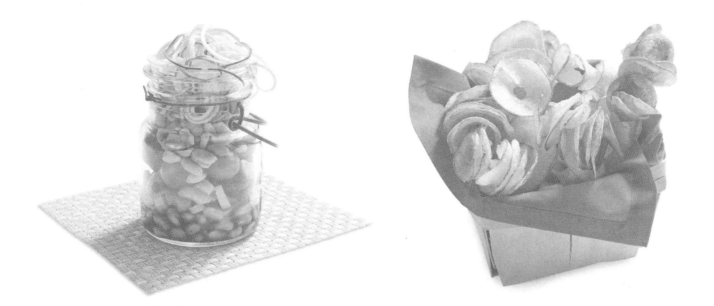

SIMPLY THE BEST
SPIRALIZER RECIPES

MARIAN GETZ

INTRODUCTION BY WOLFGANG PUCK

INTRODUCTION BY WOLFGANG PUCK

AS I LEARNED LONG AGO, ALONG

AND GRANDMOTHER, YOU SHOUL

LOTS OF LOVE INTO EVERYTHING

IS CERTAINLY EVIDENT IN THIS CO

Wolfgang Puck

THER
PUT
IS

It is often said that you eat with your eyes first. Whether in my restaurants or at home, I believe that food presentation is a big part of how we experience our meals. The Spiralizer will empower you to be more adventurous in the kitchen. Not only will you be able to prepare your food much quicker, but you will also find yourself incorporating more healthy ingredients into your family's diet while at the same time adding a colorful and decorative gourmet look that will turn a great dish into an extraordinary experience.

When I asked Marian to write the cookbook for the Spiralizer, I knew she would rise to the occasion. Her experience as a pastry chef, wife, mother, and now grandmother allowed Marian to put together a cookbook with a wide variety of recipes that I'm sure you will use for years to come.

A student of cooking is probably one of the best ways to describe Marian. She is always looking for something new, something fresh, something local, something seasonal. Her culinary knowledge combined with her passion for cooking is second to none. The recipes that Marian has written for this cookbook will motivate you to be more creative in the kitchen.

INTRODUCTION BY WOLFGANG PUCK

TABLE OF CONTENTS

SPIRALIZER TIPS

Using your Spiralizer is one of the best ways to add more fruits and vegetables to your meal. It is also very easy to do with just a few quick prep steps and the push of a button. You will undoubtably find yourself snapping pictures of the beautiful dishes you prepare using this handy kitchen tool.

PREPARING YOUR FRUITS AND VEGETABLES

Some fruits and vegetables require you to cut them in order to fit into the Spiralizer's Food Chute others naturally fit. Only spiralize fruits and vegetables when raw, not cooked. Below, please find some tips for different foods and how to best prepare them to be spiralized:

APPLES & POTATOES

Most apples and potatoes will fit into the Spiralizer's Food Chute without having to cut them. For apples, buy the pre-bagged variety as they tend to be smaller than the loose ones available at you grocery store. Most potatoes including sweet potatoes will fit although large Russet potatoes will need to be trimmed.

CARROTS

Trim and peel (or scrub) carrots before sticking the Food Grip of your Spiralizer into the center of the carrots. This will allow you to spiralize whole carrots without having to cut them into smaller pieces. When using the Narrow Ribbon or Julienne Discs, you will end up with mushroom-shaped carrot ends which are a delicious little leftover snack. Spiralized carrots also keep well for up to a week in a plastic zipper top bag.

ZUCCHINI

Simply top and tail zucchini then wash them well as they tend to be slightly sticky and often have sand adhering to the skin. Stick the Food Grip of your Spiralizer into the center of the zucchini. This will allow you to spiralize whole zucchini without having to cut them into smaller pieces. Due to the high water content of zucchini, microwaving them is a great way to heat and soften them quickly. The neutral taste of zucchini makes it a great wheat pasta replacement.

DAIKON RADISH OR GREEN RADISH

Purchase long and skinny radishes at well-stocked Asian markets as they don't require a lot of trimming to fit through the Spiralizer's Food Chute. The peppery taste of this vegetable is delicious. The Julienne or Narrow Ribbon Discs tend to work best with this vegetable.

ONIONS

It is best to buy small onions to avoid having to peel off several layers until they fit through the Spiralizer's Food Chute. Smaller onions can be found pre-bagged at the grocery store. Onions are best spiralized using the Julienne or Narrow Ribbon Discs due to the onion's wide diameter.

BROCCOLI STEMS

Instead of throwing out your broccoli stems, spiralize them as they work beautifully with the Spiralizer and taste delicious. The taste is similar to that of asparagus rather than broccoli. To spiralize the stems, trim off the woody end then use a good peeler to peel the outer skin. Sometimes broccoli stems are more tender which will allow you to skip peeling. In general, cutting the stems into 4 to 6-inch pieces works best with the Spiralizer.

BUTTERNUT SQUASH

Butternut squash is one of the most delicious vegetables to spiralize. Purchase long and skinny butternut squash as the "necks" are the only parts that are suitable for spiralizing (save remaining squash for another use). Peel the sides of the "neck" until it fits through the Spiralizer's Food Chute. Trim any thicker parts using a knife. Because of the large diameter of this vegetable, the Julienne or Narrow Ribbon Discs tend to work best.

BEETS

Beets have a tendency to stain. Wear gloves and protect your countertop and cutting board by covering them in plastic wrap before peeling or trimming.

PREPPING IN BATCHES

Preparing and cooking several meals at once is a very cost effective and time saving way to cook and the Spiralizer is the perfect tool to help you do it. Most fruits and vegetables can be spiralized and kept in containers or plastic zipper top bags for several days. Some exceptions are foods that tend to turn brown such as apples, pears and potatoes. Cucumbers also don't hold up well for longer than 1-2 days.

COOKING TIMES

In general, spiralized fruits and vegetables cook faster than their whole counterparts. Vegetable based noodles or pasta can be cooked using different methods such as steaming, boiling or using a microwave as shown in the cooking time chart on the next page. Cooking the spiralized noodles or pasta in a sauce by tossing them together in a skillet or microwaving them are the preferred methods to maximize flavor and done most often in this book. Please monitor your cooking time closely to prevent overcooking.

SPIRALIZING "NOODLES" FOR BEGINNERS

The words Pasta, Noodles, Zoodles, Zpaghetti, Zac, and Zinguini used in this book are a play on words for vegetables that are a healthier, less processed and far lower calorie pasta substitute. If you are new to vegetable pasta, mix your zoodles with some regular pasta until you are used to the different texture. The calorie savings are tremendous even if you just make it a 50/50 mixture.

VEGAN OR VEGETARIAN "MEAT" SUBSTITUTES

If you are new to vegetarianism, veganism or plant-based diets, you are in for a pleasant surprise when it comes to meat substitutes. Instead of just eating tofu, go to your grocery store's freezer section and look at the wide variety of meat substitutes available including sausage, chicken, beef and ground beef substitutes. Many of them taste very good and come precooked.

TOASTING NUTS

Toasted nuts are often used throughout this book. To toast nuts or coconut, preheat your oven to 350°F, spread nuts on a sheet pan in a single layer then toast in the oven for 10-15 minutes or until brown, crisp and fragrant.

COOKING TIME CHART

Below please find a cooking time chart for the most common spiralized vegetables using different cooking methods. Microwaving is the preferred way of cooking as it is the only method to heat the spiralized vegetables without increasing the moisture content. If you are steaming or boiling, pay close attention to the cooking time as the spiralized vegetables can easily become overcooked and mushy.

INGREDIENT	MICROWAVING	STEAMING	BOILING
Zucchini	2-3 minutes	2-3 minutes	20-30 seconds
Yellow squash	2-3 minutes	2-3 minutes	20-30 seconds
Potato	1 minute	1-2 minutes	30-50 seconds
Sweet Potato	4-5 minutes	3-5 minutes	3-5 minutes
Carrots	4-5 minutes	3-5 minutes	3-5 minutes
Daikon Radish & Green Daikon Radish	2-3 minutes	2-3 minutes	2-3 minutes
Beets	4-5 minutes	4-5 minutes	5-6 minutes
Broccoli Stem	2-3 minutes	2-3 minutes	2-3 minutes
Butternut Squash	2-3 minutes	3-4 minutes	3-4 minutes

The recipes in this cookbook are written with great taste in mind. Many recipes will contain fat, salt, cheese and sugar in order to maximize flavor. If you do not want to use those ingredients, follow the tips on the recipe pages to help you reduce, omit or substitute ingredients.

PANTRY TIPS

Being prepared to cook or bake the recipes in this book, or any recipe for that matter, is one of the keys to success in the kitchen. Your pantry must be stocked with the basics. We all know how frustrating it can be when you go to the cupboard and what you need is not there. This list includes some of the ingredients you will find in this book and some that we feel are important to always have on hand.

PERISHABLES	SPICES	DRY GOODS
Zucchini	Kosher Salt	Flours
Carrots	Fresh Peppercorn	Gluten-Free Flours
Yellow Squash	Bay Leaves	Sugar
Onions	Sage	Dates
Butternut Squash	Oregano	Honey
Apples	Thyme	Stevia Sweetener
Pears	Chili Flakes	Oils
White Potatoes	Cumin Seeds	Pickles
Sweet Potatoes	Curry Powder	Chicken Bouillon Base
Green Onions	Onion Powder	Vegetable Bouillon Base
Garlic	Garlic Powder	Canned Tomatoes
Ginger	Dry Mustard	Extracts/Flavorings
Herbs	Ground Cinnamon	Vinegars
Tomatoes	Nutmeg	
Greens	Cloves	
Milk/Almond Milk	Chili Powder	
Cheese/Vegan Cheese		
Yogurt/Non-Dairy Yogurt		
Frozen Fruits		
Frozen Vegetables		

It is not necessary to have all the items listed at all times. However, if you are feeling creative, adventurous or just following a recipe, it's great to have a good selection in the kitchen.

ZPAGHETTI &
MEATBALLS

Makes 4-5 servings

Ingredients:

1 tablespoon unsalted butter

Kosher salt and fresh pepper to taste

1 large yellow onion, finely diced

1 large carrot, finely diced

1 celery stalk, finely diced

2 garlic cloves, chopped

1 jar (32 ounces) pasta sauce

2 tablespoons heavy cream

1 branch fresh rosemary

1 tablespoon fresh oregano

12 store-bought frozen meatballs

6 large zucchini

Chopped parsley, for serving

Method:

1. *Melt the butter in a large skillet over medium-high heat.*
2. *Add remaining ingredients, except meatballs, zucchini, and parsley.*
3. *Let simmer for 10 minutes, stirring occasionally.*
4. *Add the meatballs and simmer for an additional 5 minutes.*
5. *Fit Spiralizer with the Julienne Disc.*
6. *Spiralize the zucchini then transfer to a greased 9x13-inch microwave-safe dish and sprinkle with salt.*
7. *Microwave for 3-4 minutes.*
8. *Pour the pasta sauce mixture over the zucchini.*
9. *Garnish with parsley before serving.*

TIP

To make this a vegetarian version, substitute the
meatballs with ground plant-based protein found
in the freezer section of your grocery store.

TORNADO POTATO
CHIPS

Makes 4 servings

Ingredients:

6 Yukon Gold potatoes

1 tablespoon olive oil

Kosher salt and fresh pepper to taste

1/2 teaspoon paprika

Method:

1. *Preheat oven to 275°F and line two sheet pans with parchment paper; set aside.*
2. *Fit Spiralizer with the Narrow Ribbon Disc.*
3. *Spiralize the potatoes, rinse under cold water to remove the surface starch then pat dry using paper towels.*
4. *Divide the potatoes between the sheet pans, drizzle with oil then season with salt, pepper and paprika.*
5. *Bake for 30-45 minutes or until dry and just beginning to brown.*
6. *Remove and serve.*
7. *Chips can be kept in an airtight container at room temperature for up to 1 week.*

BASIC ZOODLES

Makes 4 servings

Ingredients:

Kosher salt to taste

4 large zucchini

Olive oil to taste

Method:

1. *Bring an 8-quart stockpot of water to a boil then season with salt.*
2. *Fit Spiralizer with desired disc.*
3. *Spiralize the zucchini.*
4. *Drop zucchini into the boiling water and cook for 30 seconds.*
5. *Immediately remove from water and drain thoroughly.*
6. *Drizzle with oil then toss very gently to coat.*
7. *Garnish as desired and serve immediately.*

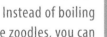

TIP

Instead of boiling the zoodles, you can microwave them for 2-3 minutes.

APPLE ROSE
TARTS

Makes 4 tarts

Ingredients:

2 small apples

1/4 cup dark brown sugar, packed

1/2 teaspoon ground cinnamon

2 tablespoons unsalted butter, melted

4 store-bought tart shells (4-inches each)

Method:

1. *Preheat oven to 475°F.*
2. *Fit Spiralizer with the Wide Ribbon Disc.*
3. *Spiralize the apples then transfer to a mixing bowl.*
4. *Add the brown sugar, cinnamon and butter then toss to combine.*
5. *Arrange apple spirals in overlapping circles so that it resembles a rose.*
6. *Neatly place a spiral into each tart shell.*
7. *Bake for 10-12 minutes or until edges of apples are brown.*
8. *Remove, garnish as desired and serve hot.*

TIP

You can make these tarts using pears to achieve a more complete spiral because pears are more pliable than apples. When you spiralize the pears they will not break and keep in one long spiral which makes these tarts look even better.

WOLF'S CARROT RAISIN SALAD

Makes 4-6 servings

Ingredients:

8 large carrots

1/2 cup dark raisins

1 cup pineapple tidbits

Kosher salt and fresh pepper to taste

1/2 cup mayonnaise

2 tablespoons yellow mustard

1 tablespoon apple cider vinegar

3 tablespoons granulated sugar

Method:

1. *Fit Spiralizer with the Narrow Ribbon Disc.*
2. *Spiralize the carrots then transfer to a mixing bowl.*
3. *Add the raisins and pineapple to the mixing bowl then season with salt and pepper.*
4. *In a separate small bowl, whisk together remaining ingredients.*
5. *Pour mayonnaise mixture over the carrot mixture and stir to combine.*
6. *Garnish as desired and serve.*

GARLIC SHRIMP & VEGGIE "PASTA"

Makes 4 servings

Ingredients:

2 Russet potatoes

4 zucchini

2 large carrots

2 tablespoons olive oil

8 ounces small shrimp

4 garlic cloves, chopped

A few sprigs fresh oregano

Kosher salt and fresh pepper to taste

1 jalapeño pepper, sliced (optional)

Method:

1. *Fit Spiralizer with the Narrow Ribbon Disc.*
2. *Spiralize the potatoes then rinse immediately under cold water to remove the surface starch.*
3. *Place potatoes on paper towels to drain.*
4. *Spiralize the zucchini and carrots then set aside.*
5. *Preheat the oil in a large skillet over medium-high heat.*
6. *Add the shrimp, garlic, and remaining ingredients including the vegetables and stir.*
7. *Cook for 2-3 minutes or until shrimp is pink and vegetables are just heated through.*
8. *Remove, garnish as desired and serve immediately.*

WOLF'S FAMOUS
CHICKEN SALAD

Makes 4 servings

Ingredients:

For the Salad:

2 large carrots

1 daikon radish or 12 radishes

1 head Napa cabbage, julienned

1 bunch green onions, sliced + more for garnish

2 cups leftover chicken, shredded

Fried wonton strips or chow mein noodles, for serving

For the Dressing:

1 tablespoon dry mustard

2 tablespoons soy sauce

1/4 cup rice wine vinegar

1/4 cup honey

1 teaspoon dark sesame oil

1/2 cup canola oil

Method:

1. Fit Spiralizer with the Julienne Disc.
2. Spiralize carrots and radishes then transfer to a mixing bowl.
3. Add the cabbage, green onions and chicken then toss to combine.
4. In a separate small bowl, whisk together all dressing ingredients, except canola oil.
5. Stream the canola oil into the mustard mixture until smooth and emulsified.
6. Pour some of the dressing over the salad and toss to combine.
7. Garnish as desired and serve with fried wonton strips and additional green onions on top.

TIP

This is my favorite salad from Wolfgang's restaurant in Santa Monica called Chinois on Main.

POTATO LATKES

Makes 10 latkes

Ingredients:

6 Russet potatoes

1 small yellow onion

Kosher salt and fresh pepper to taste

6 tablespoons unsalted butter, melted

Canola oil, for sautéing

Sour cream, applesauce and green onions, for serving

Method:

1. *Fit Spiralizer with the Julienne Disc.*
2. *Spiralize potatoes and onion then place onto a kitchen towel.*
3. *Squeeze potatoes and onions in the towel to remove as much excess moisture as possible then transfer to a mixing bowl.*
4. *Add the salt, pepper and melted butter to the mixing bowl then toss to coat.*
5. *Preheat some oil in a large skillet over medium-high heat.*
6. *Pull potato strands mixture into small piles then place as many as will fit into the skillet, patting down the tops using a spatula.*
7. *Cook for 2-3 minutes on each side or until golden brown then remove and repeat with remaining mixture.*
8. *Garnish as desired and serve with sour cream, applesauce and green onions.*

CUCUMBER TZATZIKI
SALAD

Makes 4 servings

Ingredients:

3 English cucumbers

1 cup Greek yogurt

Zest and juice of 2 lemons

Kosher salt and fresh pepper to taste

2 garlic cloves, minced

1 tablespoon mint leaves, chopped

1 teaspoon oregano leaves, chopped

Method:

1. *Fit Spiralizer with the Narrow Ribbon Disc.*
2. *Spiralize the cucumbers then transfer to a large mixing bowl.*
3. *Add remaining ingredients to the mixing bowl then stir gently to combine.*
4. *Garnish as desired and serve.*

ZOODLE JAR
SALAD

Makes 2 jars

Ingredients:

2 large zucchini

1/4 cup store-bought dressing of your choice

1/2 cup edamame, shelled

1/2 cup celery, sliced

1/2 cup raisins

1/2 cup cherry tomatoes

1/2 cup peanuts

Method:

1. *Fit Spiralizer with the Julienne Disc.*
2. *Spiralize the zucchini then set aside.*
3. *Divide remaining ingredients between two mason jars in the order listed then top with the zucchini.*
4. *When ready to eat, invert into a serving bowl and serve.*
5. *Salad can be kept in the lidded mason jars in the refrigerator for up to 3 days.*

TIP

You can experiment with vegetables other than zucchini to make different salads. See the tips section starting on page 6 for examples of vegetables that are great to spiralize.

QUINOA BEET
SALAD

Makes 4-6 servings

Ingredients:

2 cups quinoa, cooked and cooled

1/2 cup brine from a jar of pepperoncini peppers

1/4 cup pepperoncini peppers, sliced

2 cups fresh baby spinach

1/4 cup extra-virgin olive oil

1/2 cup Swiss cheese, diced

Kosher salt and fresh pepper to taste

1/2 cup golden raisins

1/2 cup smoked almonds

2 small beets

Method:

1. Combine all ingredients, except beets, in a mixing bowl; toss to coat.
2. Fit Spiralizer with the Julienne Disc.
3. Spiralize the beets then rinse under cold water to remove surface color.
4. Using scissors, cut beets into roughly 2-inch lengths.
5. Add beets to the quinoa mixture, toss quickly then transfer to a serving bowl (do not toss too much or the whole salad will turn pink).
6. Garnish as desired and serve.

STEAK, KALE & CARROT
SALAD

Makes 4 servings

Ingredients:

- large carrots
- tablespoon olive oil
- small sirloin or strip steaks
- Kosher salt and fresh pepper to taste
- /3 cup bottled oil & vinegar dressing
- bunch kale, finely julienned

Method:

1. *Fit Spiralizer with the Julienne Disc.*
2. *Spiralize the carrots then set aside.*
3. *Preheat the olive oil in a large skillet over medium-high heat.*
4. *Season steaks with salt and pepper then add to the hot skillet.*
5. *Cook for a few minutes on each side or until desired doneness; remove and let rest.*
6. *Immediately add the dressing, kale and carrots to the hot skillet; toss until wilted then remove from skillet and pour the juices over the greens.*
7. *Cut steaks into thin slices and serve with the wilted salad.*
8. *Garnish as desired and serve hot.*

CHICKEN ZOODLES WITH
PEANUT SAUCE

Makes 4 servings

Ingredients:

4 large zucchini

1 large carrot

2 cups leftover chicken, shredded

1/2 cup coconut milk or chicken stock

Soy sauce to taste

1/2 cup jarred peanut sauce

3 garlic cloves, minced

Chopped cilantro, sriracha and crushed peanuts, for serving

Method:

1. *Fit Spiralizer with the Wide Ribbon Disc.*
2. *Spiralize the zucchini and carrot then transfer to a microwave-safe bowl.*
3. *Add remaining ingredients except cilantro, sriracha and peanuts, stir then microwave for 3-4 minutes or until hot.*
4. *Serve with cilantro, sriracha and crushed peanuts.*

ZAC &
CHEESE

Makes 4-5 servings

Ingredients:

10 ounces extra-sharp Cheddar cheese, cubed

2/3 cup mozzarella cheese, cubed

3 ounces Parmesan cheese, cubed

1 1/2 cups whole milk

1/4 cup all-purpose flour

1/2 small white onion, cut into chunks

1/4 teaspoon freshly ground black pepper

1 teaspoon kosher salt

1/2 teaspoon dry mustard powder

8 zucchini or as needed

Method:

1. *Place all ingredients, except zucchini, into a high powered blender.*
2. *Cover and blend on high speed for 4 minutes or until cheese sauce is steamy and hot.*
3. *Fit Spiralizer with the Julienne Disc.*
4. *Spiralize enough zucchini to make 8 cups then transfer to a serving dish.*
5. *Pour hot cheese sauce over the zucchini, stir to combine then let rest for 5 minutes.*
6. *Garnish as desired and serve.*

GREEK SKILLET
SUPPER

Makes 2-4 servings

Ingredients:

3 small beets, peeled

1 small red onion

1/2 cup cherry tomatoes

1 tablespoon garlic, chopped

2 teaspoons fresh oregano

1 tablespoon red wine vinegar

1/3 cup Kalamata olives

1 tablespoon olive oil

Kosher salt and fresh pepper to taste

4 ounces feta cheese, crumbled

4 large basil leaves, for serving

Method:

1. *Preheat oven to 400°F.*
2. *Fit Spiralizer with the Julienne Disc.*
3. *Spiralize the beets and onion then transfer to a large mixing bowl.*
4. *Add remaining ingredients, except feta cheese and basil, to the mixing bowl and toss to combine.*
5. *Pour mixture into a greased oven-safe dish then cover with aluminum foil.*
6. *Bake for 20 minutes, remove foil, sprinkle feta cheese over the top then bake uncovered for an additional 5-8 minutes.*
7. *Remove, top with basil, garnish as desired and serve.*

BUDDHA
BOWL

Makes 4 bowls

Ingredients:

For the Bowl:

large carrots

English cucumber

/2 cup crab meat or imitation crab

avocado, sliced

For Serving:

Hot rice, cooked

Pickled ginger

Soy sauce

Wasabi

Sesame seeds

Method:

1. *Fit Spiralizer with the Julienne Disc.*
2. *Spiralize the carrots and cucumber then divide between four bowls.*
3. *Divide the crab and avocado between the four bowls.*
4. *Serve with rice, pickled ginger, soy sauce, wasabi and sesame seeds.*

TIP

When you take a bite of all the bowl ingredients together, it tastes just like a California sushi roll.

PLAIN POTATO "PASTA"

Makes 4 servings

Ingredients:

8 medium Yukon Gold or Russet potatoes

Kosher salt to taste

Olive oil to taste

Method:

1. *Bring an 8-quart stockpot of water to a boil and season with salt.*
2. *Fit Spiralizer with the Julienne Disc.*
3. *Spiralize the potatoes.*
4. *Rinse potatoes immediately under cold water to remove the surface starch.*
5. *Drop potatoes into the boiling water and cook for 30 to 60 seconds or until "pasta" is al dente then remove immediately.*
6. *Drizzle with oil and toss very gently to coat.*
7. *Garnish as desired and serve immediately.*

TIP

It is important not to overcook the "pasta" or you will end up with mashed potatoes.

VEGGIE PASTA FOR
BEGINNERS

Makes 4 servings

Ingredients:

4 zucchini, peeled if desired

1 tablespoon olive oil

1 tablespoon unsalted butter

4 garlic cloves, chopped

Kosher salt, fresh pepper and chili flakes to taste

1 pound spaghetti, cooked and hot

Block of Parmesan cheese, for serving

Method:

1. *Fit Spiralizer with the Julienne Disc.*
2. *Spiralize the zucchini then set aside.*
3. *Preheat the oil and butter in a large skillet over medium-high heat.*
4. *Add the garlic, salt, pepper and chili flakes then stir until fragrant.*
5. *Add the spiralized zucchini and spaghetti then stir gently for 2-3 minutes or until just heated through.*
6. *Remove then grate some Parmesan cheese over the top before serving.*

TIP

If you are new to zucchini noodles or "zoodles", this recipe is the best way to start because it still has the taste and texture of pasta. As you get used to it and like the taste, gradually reduce the amount of spaghetti used until you are just using zoodles.

CARROT CAKE

Makes one 8-inch layer cake

Ingredients:

4 large carrots

2 large eggs

1/2 cup vegetable oil

1 1/3 cup sugar + more for garnish

1/2 cup pureed pineapple

1 1/2 teaspoons kosher salt

1 tablespoon ground cinnamon

2 cups unbleached all purpose flour

1 teaspoon baking soda

1 teaspoon baking powder

2 teaspoons vanilla extract

1 can store-bought cream cheese icing

Method:

1. *Preheat oven to 350°F.*
2. *Fit Spiralizer with the Julienne Disc.*
3. *Spiralize the carrots, set aside a handful for garnish, cut remaining carrots into short lengths using scissors then transfer to a mixing bowl.*
4. *Add remaining ingredients, except icing, to the mixing bowl then whisk to combine.*
5. *Pour batter into two 8-inch greased round pans.*
6. *Bake for 25 minutes or until cake springs back when touched in the center.*
7. *Toss reserved carrots in additional sugar.*
8. *Allow cake to cool completely before icing.*
9. *Fill and frost the cake with icing then top with sugared carrots before serving.*

TIP

For a healthier carrot cake, you can replace all of the sugar and oil with 1 cup pitted medjool dates and 1 1/2 cups water pureed in a high-speed blender then added to the rest of the ingredients in step 4. The texture of the cake will slightly change but it will still be delicious.

RECIPES

~SY ~ACOS

~~es 4 servings

Ingredients:

For the Tacos:

1 large carrot

6 large radishes

1 small red onion

1 small jicama bulb (optional)

1/2 cup chicken stock

2 cups leftover meat such as chicken, shredded

Kosher salt and fresh pepper to taste

For Serving:

2 cups green cabbage, shredded

12 corn or flour tortillas

Tomatoes, sliced

Avocado, sliced

Jalapeño peppers, sliced

Lime wedges

Method:

1. *Fit Spiralizer with the Julienne Disc.*
2. *Spiralize the carrot, radishes, red onion and jicama; keep each in a separate bowl.*
3. *Pour chicken stock into a skillet over medium-high heat then add the chicken.*
4. *Season with salt and pepper, simmer until hot then transfer chicken to a serving dish.*
5. *Arrange all ingredients so that everyone can build their own tacos as desired.*

ENCHILADA
BAKE

Makes 4 servings

Ingredients:

6 large carrots

1 small white onion

4 corn tortillas, torn

1 package (2 ounces) enchilada seasoning

2 cups leftover chicken, shredded

1 cup corn kernels

1 can (17 ounces) enchilada sauce

1 cup Monterrey jack cheese, shredded

Kosher salt and fresh pepper to taste

Chopped cilantro, for serving

Method:

1. *Preheat oven to 400°F and butter a baking dish; set aside.*
2. *Fit Spiralizer with the Julienne Disc.*
3. *Spiralize the carrots and onion.*
4. *Press the carrots and onion into the baking dish, tearing any carrots that are too long.*
5. *Top carrots with remaining ingredients, except cheese, salt, pepper and cilantro.*
6. *Top with cheese then season with salt and pepper.*
7. *Bake for 25-30 minutes or until brown and bubbly.*
8. *Remove, top with cilantro, garnish as desired and serve hot.*

ZUCCHINI ALFREDO WITH
CHICKEN

Makes 5-6 servings

Ingredients:

1 package (8 ounces) cream cheese, softened

1 cup Parmesan cheese, grated

1/2 cup dry white wine

Kosher salt and fresh pepper to taste

1 cup whole milk

1 cup mozzarella cheese, grated

2 cups leftover rotisserie chicken, chopped

6 large zucchini

Method:

1. *Place the cream cheese, Parmesan cheese, wine, salt and pepper into a large microwave-safe bowl then use a hand mixer to combine.*
2. *Add the milk and mozzarella cheese until blended.*
3. *Add the chicken and stir using a rubber spatula.*
4. *Microwave for 6-8 minutes or until bubbly.*
5. *Fit the Spiralizer with the Wide Ribbon Disc.*
6. *Spiralize the zucchini then transfer to a serving dish.*
7. *Pour cheese mixture over the zucchini and let stand for 5 minutes.*
8. *Garnish as desired and serve.*

BEEF & BROCCOLI
STIR-FRY

Makes 4 servings

Ingredients:

4 broccoli stems, peeled if woody (see tips on page 7)

2 tablespoons vegetable oil

4 garlic cloves, minced

4 coins fresh ginger, minced

4 cups broccoli florets

1 red bell pepper, sliced

6 ounces beef sirloin, thinly sliced

1/4 cup beef stock

1/4 cup oyster sauce

2 tablespoons hoisin sauce

Soy sauce, to taste

Method:

1. *Fit Spiralizer with the Julienne Disc.*
2. *Spiralize the broccoli stems then set aside.*
3. *Preheat the oil in a large skillet over high heat.*
4. *Add the garlic, ginger, broccoli florets, bell pepper and beef to the skillet and toss well.*
5. *Cook for 2-3 minutes or until beef is no longer red.*
6. *Add remaining ingredients as well as the spiralized broccoli stem "pasta".*
7. *Toss until everything is well coated with the sauce.*
8. *Remove, garnish as desired and serve hot.*

CRISPY PEAR
STRINGS

Makes 4 servings

Ingredients:

4 firm pears such as Bosc

2 tablespoons granulated sugar

1/4 teaspoon ground nutmeg

1/2 teaspoon ground cinnamon

1/2 teaspoon freeze dried vanilla (optional)

Pinch of kosher salt

Method:

1. *Preheat oven to 275°F and line two sheet pans with parchment paper; set aside.*
2. *Fit Spiralizer with the Julienne Disc.*
3. *Spiralize the pears then transfer to a large mixing bowl.*
4. *Sprinkle pears with sugar, nutmeg, cinnamon, vanilla and salt then toss gently using your hands.*
5. *Loosely pile pears onto sheet pans and distribute evenly.*
6. *Bake for 30-45 minutes or until dry and beginning to brown.*
7. *Pear strings can be stored in an airtight container at room temperature for up to 1 week.*

TIP
For a healthier snack, you can omit the sugar and the strings will still be sweet and delicious.

APPLE PEAR
PARFAITS

Makes 4 servings

Ingredients:

- 1 small apple, such as Honey Crisp
- 1 small, firm pear
- 2 cups store-bought rice pudding
- 1/4 cup toasted pecans, chopped (see toasting tips on page 7)
- 1 cup raspberries

Method:

1. *Fit Spiralizer with the Julienne Disc.*
2. *Spiralize the apple and pear.*
3. *Layer apple, pear, rice pudding, pecans and raspberries into parfait glasses.*
4. *Garnish as desired and serve.*

TIP

For a healthier version, you can substitute yogurt or even vegan yogurt for the rice pudding.

STUFFED PORTOBELLO CAPS

Makes 4 servings

Ingredients:

1 small yellow onion

1 large carrot

1 Russet potato

2 tablespoons olive oil

4 garlic cloves

Kosher salt and fresh pepper to taste

1 teaspoon paprika

1 tablespoons red wine vinegar

1 cup mozzarella cheese, shredded

4 large Portobello mushrooms, stemmed

TIP

For crispier cups, use a teaspoon to scrape out the black gills on the underside of the mushrooms. The gills contain a lot of water which makes the caps softer.

Method:

1. Preheat oven to 400°F and line a sheet pan with parchment paper; set aside.
2. Fit Spiralizer with the Julienne Disc.
3. Spiralize the onion, carrot and potato.
4. Preheat the oil in a large skillet over medium-high heat.
5. Add the garlic, spiralized vegetables, salt and pepper to the skillet then stir for 5 minutes or until wilted and softened.
6. Add the paprika and vinegar then remove from heat and add the cheese.
7. Place mushroom caps onto the sheet pan then season with salt and pepper.
8. Divide vegetable mixture between the mushroom caps.
9. Bake for 15-20 minutes or until brown and bubbly.
10. Remove, garnish as desired and serve.

CHICKEN PESTO "PASTA"

Makes 4 servings

Ingredients:

1 sweet potato

2 turnips

1 English cucumber

1 small yellow onion

1 tablespoon olive oil

Kosher salt, fresh pepper and chili flakes to taste

2 chicken breasts, cooked and sliced

1/2 cup jarred pesto sauce

Method:

1. *Fit Spiralizer with the Narrow Ribbon Disc.*
2. *Spiralize the potato, turnips, cucumber and onion; set aside.*
3. *Preheat the oil in a large skillet over medium-high heat.*
4. *Add the vegetables then season with salt, pepper and chili flakes.*
5. *Add remaining ingredients, toss to coat and cook until warmed through.*
6. *Remove, garnish as desired and serve hot.*

BEET, BLUE CHEESE & ORANGE SALAD

Makes 4-6 servings

Ingredients:

1 small red onion

5 small raw beets, peeled

1/2 cup store-bought balsamic vinaigrette

Kosher salt and fresh pepper to taste

3 tablespoons honey

1/2 cup pecans, toasted (see toasting tips on page 7)

1/3 cup blue cheese, crumbled

2 oranges, segmented

Method:

1. *Fit Spiralizer with the Julienne Disc.*
2. *Spiralize the onion and beets then transfer to a serving bowl.*
3. *Pat down beets and onions into an even layer.*
4. *In a separate bowl, whisk together the vinaigrette, salt, pepper and honey then drizzle evenly over beet mixture.*
5. *Scatter remaining ingredients evenly over the beets.*
6. *Garnish as desired and serve.*

RANCH SWEET POTATO WISPS

Makes 4 servings

Ingredients:

4 sweet potatoes

2 tablespoons olive oil

1 package (2 ounces) dry ranch dressing mix

Method:

1. Preheat oven to 275°F and line two sheet pans with parchment paper; set aside.
2. Fit Spiralizer with the Julienne Disc.
3. Spiralize the sweet potatoes then transfer to a large mixing bowl.
4. Sprinkle oil and some ranch dressing mix over the potatoes then toss gently using your hands.
5. Loosely pile the sweet potatoes onto the sheet pans and distribute evenly.
6. Bake for 30-45 minutes or until dry, crispy and beginning to brown.
7. Remove, garnish as desired and serve or may be stored in an airtight container at room temperature for up to 1 week.

QUICK CUCUMBER PICKLES

Makes 4 cups

Ingredients:

2 English cucumbers

1 small yellow onion

1 tablespoon pickling spice

1/2 cup apple cider vinegar

1 cup ice cubes

1 tablespoon kosher salt

3 tablespoons granulated sugar

Method:

1. *Fit Spiralizer with the Wide Ribbon Disc.*
2. *Spiralize the cucumbers then transfer to a storage container.*
3. *In a mixing bowl, stir together remaining ingredients then pour over the cucumbers.*
4. *Chill for 20 minutes before serving or store in the refrigerator for up to 1 week.*

CHILI
ZAC

Makes 4 servings

Ingredients:

For the Chili Zac:

4 large zucchini

1 tablespoon olive oil

1 pound lean beef or turkey, coarsely ground

Kosher salt, fresh pepper and chili flakes to taste

1 large yellow onion, chopped

6 garlic cloves, chopped

1 teaspoon ground cumin

4 tablespoons chili powder

2 tablespoons beef bouillon paste

1 can (28 ounces) diced tomatoes

1 can (6 ounces) tomato paste

4 corn tortillas, torn into small pieces

For Serving:

Sour cream

Cheddar cheese, shredded

Cilantro

TIP

You can easily turn this into a vegetarian version using ground plant-based protein found in the freezer section of your grocery store as well using vegetable bouillon paste, vegan sour cream and cheese.

Method:

1. *Fit Spiralizer with the Julienne Disc.*
2. *Spiralize the zucchini then set aside.*
3. *Place the oil, meat, salt, pepper and chili flakes into a large saucepan over medium heat.*
4. *Stir to break up the meat then add remaining Chili Zac ingredients, except zucchini.*
5. *Reduce heat to low and simmer for 15 minutes, stirring often.*
6. *Place zucchini into a microwave-safe bowl then season with salt.*
7. *Microwave for 5 minutes or until hot and steamy.*
8. *Serve chili on top of zucchini "noodles" then top with sour cream, cheese and cilantro.*

CARROT ENDIVE
GOAT CHEESE CUPS

Makes 8-10 servings

Ingredients:

2 large carrots

Kosher salt and fresh pepper to taste

4 ounces goat cheese

1 teaspoon lemon zest

1 tablespoon lemon juice

2 garlic cloves, minced

1/4 teaspoon thyme leaves

6 Belgian endives, separated into petals

Honey, for drizzling

Method:

1. *Fit Spiralizer with the Julienne Disc.*
2. *Spiralize the carrots then transfer to a mixing bowl, reserving some carrots for garnish.*
3. *Season carrots with salt and pepper and let stand for 10 minutes to soften.*
4. *In a small bowl, stir together the goat cheese, lemon zest, juice, garlic and thyme.*
5. *Stir the cheese mixture into the carrots then season with additional salt and pepper to taste.*
6. *Arrange endive petals on a serving platter.*
7. *Using clean hands, roll up balls of goat cheese mixture then place onto endive petals.*
8. *Sprinkle the cups with pepper, garnish with reserved carrots then drizzle with honey right before serving.*

APPLE SALAD

Makes 4 servings

Ingredients:

4 small apples

1/4 cup raisins

1/4 cup pecans

1 can (10 ounces) pineapple tidbits, drained

1/2 cup mandarin oranges

1/4 cup maraschino cherries, thoroughly drained

1/2 cup mini marshmallows

1/4 cup sour cream

1/4 cup mayonnaise

1/4 cup granulated sugar

1 tablespoon lemon juice

Kosher salt and fresh pepper to taste

Method:

1. *Fit Spiralizer with the Narrow Ribbon Disc.*
2. *Spiralize the apples then transfer to a mixing bowl.*
3. *Add remaining ingredients to the bowl, season with salt and pepper then stir to combine.*
4. *Transfer to a serving bowl, garnish as desired and serve.*

BACON "PASTA" SKILLET
SUPPER

Makes 4 servings

Ingredients:

4 large zucchini

8 bacon slices, chopped

1 small yellow onion, diced

1 package (8 ounces) cream cheese

1/3 cup chicken stock

1/4 cup Parmesan cheese, grated

Kosher salt and fresh pepper to taste

Method:

1. *Fit Spiralizer with the Julienne Disc.*
2. *Spiralize the zucchini then set aside.*
3. *Preheat a large skillet over medium-high heat then add the bacon.*
4. *Stir bacon until they begin to brown then add the onions and cook for a few minutes until onions are translucent.*
5. *Add the cream cheese, stock, Parmesan, salt and pepper; stir until smooth.*
6. *Add the zucchini then stir just to combine.*
7. *Let cook until zucchini are heated through.*
8. *Remove, garnish as desired and serve hot.*

LIGHTER CHICKEN
NOODLE SOUP

Makes 8 cups

Ingredients:

1 quart chicken stock

4 chicken breasts or thighs, raw

4 large carrots

2 small yellow onions

2 parsnips

1 cup celery, chopped

3 garlic cloves, chopped

1 bay leaf

Kosher salt and fresh pepper to taste

Method:

1. *Pour stock into a stockpot with the chicken and bring to a simmer over medium-high heat.*
2. *Fit Spiralizer with the Narrow Ribbon Disc.*
3. *Spiralize the carrots, onions and parsnips then transfer to the stockpot.*
4. *Add remaining ingredients to the stockpot and let simmer for 20-30 minutes.*
5. *Garnish as desired and serve hot.*

TIP

This soup is significantly lighter than typical chicken noodle soup as it does not contain any added fats or wheat pasta.

POTATO EGG CUPS

Makes 6 servings

Ingredients:

4 Yukon gold potatoes, peeled

Kosher salt and fresh pepper to taste

4 tablespoons unsalted butter

6 eggs

Chopped parsley, for serving

TIP

For lower calorie cups, you can use egg whites instead of whole eggs. The kind from the carton sold at the grocery store work fine as well.

Method:

1. Preheat oven to 400°F.
2. Fit the Spiralizer with the Julienne Disc.
3. Spiralize the potatoes then transfer to a mixing bowl.
4. Sprinkle potatoes with salt and pepper then toss and let rest for 5 minutes.
5. Evenly divide the potatoes between the wells of a muffin tin.
6. Bake for 10 minutes or until potato edges are a little crispy.
7. Remove from oven, crack an egg into each well then season with additional salt and pepper.
8. Return to oven and bake for an additional 10-12 minutes or until egg is cooked to desired doneness.
9. Top with parsley, garnish as desired and serve.

BUTTERNUT SQUASH
SALAD

Makes 4-6 servings

Ingredients:

2 butternut squash, neck only, peeled (see tips on page 7)

1/2 cup bottled Italian dressing

1/4 cup honey

2 tablespoons Dijon mustard

Kosher salt and fresh pepper to taste

1/2 cup blue cheese, crumbled

1/2 cup toasted hazelnuts, chopped (see toasting tips on page 7)

1/2 cup celery, chopped

1/2 cup fresh, frozen or dried cranberries

2 tablespoons fresh parsley, chopped

Method:

1. *Fit Spiralizer with the Wide Ribbon Disc.*
2. *Trim butternut squash necks to fit through the Spiralizer's Food Chute (see tips on page 7).*
3. *Spiralize the butternut squash then transfer to a mixing bowl.*
4. *In a separate small bowl, whisk together the dressing, honey, mustard salt and pepper.*
5. *Pour dressing mixture over the butternut squash, toss to coat then let stand for 10 minutes to soften.*
6. *Add remaining ingredients and toss to combine.*
7. *Garnish as desired and serve.*

CUCUMBER CREAM CHEESE
TEA SANDWICHES

Makes 4 servings

Ingredients:

1 English cucumber
1 tub (8 ounces) vegetable-flavored cream cheese
4 whole grain bread slices

Method:

1. *Fit Spiralizer with the Wide Ribbon Disc.*
2. *Spiralize the cucumbers then set aside.*
3. *Spread cream cheese onto bread slices then trim crusts if desired.*
4. *Top each sandwich with cucumber ribbons.*
5. *Cut into fingers, squares or leave slices whole.*
6. *Garnish as desired and serve.*

TIP

Use any flavor cream
cheese you like.

BEET RIBBON SALAD WITH SALMON

Makes 4 servings

Ingredients:

6 small raw beets, peeled

Zest and juice of 2 lemons

2 tablespoons olive oil

2 tablespoons honey

Kosher salt and fresh pepper to taste

2 tablespoons fresh dill, chopped

3 ounces smoked salmon

Sour cream and additional dill, for serving

Method:

1. *Fit Spiralizer with the Narrow Ribbon Disc.*
2. *Spiralize the beets then transfer to a mixing bowl.*
3. *Add the lemon zest and juice, oil, honey, salt, pepper and dill.*
4. *Toss to combine then divide between serving plates.*
5. *Serve with salmon, sour cream and dill.*

AHI TUNA SALAD

Makes 2 servings

Ingredients:

2 zucchini

1 carrot

1 daikon radish

2 tablespoons red wine vinegar

Kosher salt and fresh pepper to taste

1/4 cup store-bought chimichurri sauce or pesto

2 tablespoons olive oil

2 small sushi grade tuna steaks

Method:

1. *Fit Spiralizer with the Julienne Disc.*
2. *Spiralize the zucchini, carrot and daikon radish then transfer to a mixing bowl.*
3. *Add vinegar, salt, pepper and chimichurri sauce to the bowl; stir well then set aside.*
4. *Preheat the oil in a small skillet over medium-high heat.*
5. *Season tuna steaks with salt and pepper then place into the skillet.*
6. *Cook for 20-30 seconds on all sides for a very rare fish then remove from the skillet.*
7. *Toss the salad then divide between two bowls.*
8. *Slice tuna then place on top of salad.*
9. *Garnish as desired and serve.*

TIP

If you are not into tuna, you can use a cooked chicken breast or plant-based protein instead.

CHOCOLATE SWEET POTATO
MUFFINS

Makes 12 muffins

Ingredients:

1 sweet potato

1 cup unsalted butter, softened

1 cup light brown sugar, packed

4 large eggs

1 tablespoon vanilla extract

2/3 cup cocoa powder

2 teaspoons baking soda

1/2 teaspoon kosher salt

2 cups all purpose flour

1 cup water

1 1/2 cups sour cream

1 cup chocolate chips

Method:

1. *Fit Spiralizer with the Julienne Disc.*
2. *Spiralize the sweet potato then set aside.*
3. *Preheat oven to 350°F and prepare a cupcake pan with papers; set aside.*
4. *In a mixing bowl, cream the butter and sugar using a hand mixer until fluffy.*
5. *Add the eggs, one at a time, then add the vanilla and mix until smooth.*
6. *Sift the cocoa powder, baking soda, salt and flour then add to the mixing bowl while alternating with water and sour cream using low mixing speed.*
7. *Cut the sweet potatoes into short lengths using scissors then add to the batter.*
8. *Add chocolate chips and mix until just smooth.*
9. *Using an ice cream scoop, fill each cupcake paper 3/4 full of batter.*
10. *Bake for about 20-25 minutes or puffed and set.*
11. *Remove and serve warm.*

TIP

The sweet potatoes in this recipe make these muffins extra moist and delicious.

CURRIED CARROT "PASTA"

Makes 4 servings

Ingredients:

8 large carrots

2 tablespoons coconut or olive oil

3 garlic cloves, chopped

1 tablespoon fresh ginger, chopped

Kosher salt and fresh pepper to taste

2 teaspoons curry powder

1/4 cup dark raisins

1 cup pineapple tidbits

Chopped cilantro, for serving

Method:

1. *Fit Spiralizer with the Narrow Ribbon Disc.*
2. *Spiralize the carrots then set aside.*
3. *Preheat the oil in a large skillet over medium-high heat.*
4. *Add the garlic and ginger to the skillet then stir until fragrant.*
5. *Add the carrot ribbons, season with salt and pepper then stir to coat.*
6. *Add remaining ingredients, except cilantro, then stir just until heated through.*
7. *Remove, garnish with cilantro and serve.*

APPLE, HAZELNUT &
CRANBERRY SALAD

Makes 4 servings

Ingredients:

4 small apples, such as Honey Crisp

1/2 cup celery, chopped

1/4 cup toasted hazelnuts, chopped (see toasting tips on page 7)

1/3 cup dried cranberries

1 cup pretzels, crushed

1/2 cup mayonnaise

2 tablespoons honey

2 tablespoons apple cider vinegar

Method:

1. *Fit Spiralizer with the Julienne Disc.*
2. *Spiralize apples then transfer to a mixing bowl.*
3. *Add remaining ingredients and stir to combine.*
4. *Pour into a serving bowl then garnish as desired and serve.*

CRISPY SHOESTRING
POTATOES

RECIPES

Makes 4 servings

Ingredients:

4 Russet potatoes

1 tablespoon olive oil

Kosher salt and fresh pepper to taste

A few sprigs rosemary and thyme

Method:

1. *Preheat oven to 275°F and line two sheet pans with parchment paper; set aside.*
2. *Fit Spiralizer with the Julienne Disc.*
3. *Spiralize the potatoes then transfer to a large mixing bowl.*
4. *Add remaining ingredients and toss gently using your hands.*
5. *Loosely pile potatoes onto sheet pans and distribute evenly.*
6. *Bake for 30-45 minutes or until dry and beginning to brown.*
7. *Remove, garnish as desired and serve.*

TIP

These shoestring potatoes can also be deep fried. Heat a large pan of oil such as canola to 350°F using a thermometer. Fry them in batches for 2-3 minutes or until golden brown. Always season with salt immediately after frying. For a more golden brown potato, rinse under cold water before frying to remove the surface starch from the potatoes. Pat dry before frying.

BROCCOLI STEM SLAW

Makes 4-6 servings

Ingredients:

6 broccoli stems, peeled if woody (see tips on page 7)

2 large carrots

4 large radishes

1 small apple

1/4 cup mayonnaise

1/4 cup sour cream

1/4 cup granulated sugar

2 tablespoons yellow mustard

2 tablespoons apple cider vinegar

Kosher salt and fresh pepper to taste

Method:

1. *Fit Spiralizer with the Julienne Disc.*
2. *Spiralize the broccoli stems, carrots, radishes and apple then transfer to a mixing bowl.*
3. *In a separate small bowl, whisk together remaining ingredients until smooth then pour over the broccoli stem mixture and stir to combine.*
4. *Garnish as desired and serve.*

CAPRESE ZUCCHINI SALAD

Makes 1 salad

Ingredients:

2 large zucchini

1 small red onion

2 cups small mixed tomatoes, halved or sliced

1 cup fresh mozzarella pearls

Fresh basil, chopped

Extra-virgin olive oil, for serving

Kosher salt and fresh pepper to taste

Balsamic glaze, for serving

Method:

1. *Fit Spiralizer with the Julienne Disc.*
2. *Spiralize the zucchini and red onion then transfer to a serving platter.*
3. *Scatter the tomatoes and mozzarella pearls over the zucchini and onions.*
4. *Top with the basil, olive oil, salt, pepper and balsamic glaze.*
5. *Garnish as desired and serve.*

EGG FOO YONG

Makes 8 pancakes

Ingredients:

3 large carrots

1 daikon radish or 8 regular radishes

1 small yellow onion

4 broccoli stems, peeled if woody (see tips on page 7)

1 cup leftover chicken or ham, chopped

1/2 of a small green cabbage, thinly sliced

6 large eggs

2 tablespoons cornstarch

4 garlic cloves, minced

4 coins fresh ginger, minced

Soy sauce to taste

2 teaspoons dark sesame oil

Vegetable oil, for sautéing

Method:

1. *Fit Spiralizer with the Julienne Disc.*
2. *Spiralize the carrots, radishes, onion and broccoli stems then transfer to a mixing bowl.*
3. *Add the chicken or ham to the bowl.*
4. *In a separate small bowl, whisk together remaining ingredients, except vegetable oil, then pour over vegetables and stir to combine.*
5. *Preheat vegetable oil in a large skillet over medium-high heat.*
6. *Place as many mounds as will fit into the skillet, making sure some egg is drizzled over.*
7. *Press down using a spatula and cook for 2 minutes on each side or until brown and set.*
8. *Garnish as desired and serve with additional soy sauce.*

TIP

This is a great recipe for using up leftovers that you
have in the refrigerator or freezer such as corn, peas,
green beans, broccoli or bean sprouts.

KALEIDOSCOPE
SALAD

Makes 4-6 servings

Ingredients:

2 small beets

2 large carrots

2 broccoli stems, peeled if woody (see tips on page 7)

2 small turnips

1 small rutabaga

1 small jicama

Kosher salt and fresh pepper to taste

1/2 cup bottled dressing of your choice

1/2 cup almonds, toasted (see toasting tips on page 7)

1 cup orange segments

RECIPES

Method:

1. *Fit Spiralizer with the Julienne Disc.*
2. *Spiralize the beets then place strands in cold water to remove surface color and rinse the Spiralizer.*
3. *Spiralize the carrots, broccoli stems, turnips, rutabaga and jicama then transfer to a mixing bowl and add remaining ingredients, except beets; toss to combine.*
4. *Place into a serving bowl then drain beets thoroughly and pile on top of salad.*
5. *Garnish as desired and serve.*

TIP

To serve the salad as pictured, arrange the spiralized vegetables separately on a platter, whisk all dressing ingredients together then drizzle over salad and top with oranges and almonds.

EASY "LASAGNA"

Makes 4-6 servings

Ingredients:

6 large zucchini

1 jar (32 ounces) pasta sauce

1 bag (9.6 ounces) precooked hearty sausage crumbles

1 container (24 ounces) ricotta cheese

1 cup Parmesan cheese, grated

18 Provolone cheese slices

Kosher salt and fresh pepper to taste

Method:

1. *Preheat oven to 400°F.*
2. *Fit Spiralizer with the Wide Ribbon Disc.*
3. *Spiralize the zucchini.*
4. *Grease a 9x13-inch oven-safe dish then pour 1/3 of the pasta sauce into the bottom of the dish.*
5. *Add a layer of zucchini, sausage, ricotta, Parmesan and Provolone then repeat 3 times to make additional layers.*
6. *Season with salt and pepper then bake for 25-30 minutes or until golden brown.*
7. *Remove, garnish as desired and serve.*

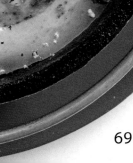

SHRIMP LETTUCE CUPS

Makes 12 lettuce cups

Ingredients:

4 large carrots

4 large radishes

2 broccoli stems, peeled if woody (see tips on page 7)

12 butter lettuce leaves

12 iceberg lettuce leaves

3 tablespoons vegetable oil

1 pound small shrimp

1 tablespoon garlic, chopped

1 bunch green onions, chopped

1 cup white mushrooms, chopped

Kosher salt and fresh pepper to taste

Hoisin sauce and sriracha hot sauce, for serving

TIP

You can add the spiralized veggies to the skillet for a few minutes if you prefer them to be hot and softer.

Method:

1. *Fit Spiralizer with the Julienne Disc.*
2. *Spiralize carrots, radishes and broccoli stems.*
3. *Place butter lettuce leaves inside iceberg cups then arrange on a platter.*
4. *Top lettuce cups with the spiralized vegetables; set aside.*
5. *Preheat a large skillet over high heat then add the oil, shrimp, garlic, green onions and mushrooms.*
6. *Stir, season with salt and pepper then cook for about 5 minutes or until shrimp is pink.*
7. *Remove from heat then divide mixture between the lettuce cups.*
8. *Garnish as desired and serve topped with hoisin sauce and sriracha.*

BTZ (BACON, TOMATO, ZUCCHINI) SALAD

Makes 4 servings

Ingredients:

4 zucchini

2 carrots

12 bacon slices, cooked and chopped

4 small tomatoes, sliced

Kosher salt and fresh pepper to taste

Mayonnaise, for serving

Method:

1. *Fit Spiralizer with the Julienne Disc.*
2. *Spiralize the zucchini and carrots.*
3. *Arrange zucchini and carrots on a serving platter.*
4. *Arrange the bacon and tomatoes on top then season with salt and pepper.*
5. *Garnish as desired and serve with a bit of mayonnaise.*

TIP

You can use turkey bacon or even vegan bacon for this salad. For a lighter dish, substitute the mayonnaise with Greek yogurt.

BEET RUFFLE
CHIPS

Makes 4 servings

Ingredients:

6 medium raw beets, peeled

3 tablespoons olive oil

2 garlic cloves, shaved

A few sprigs rosemary

A few sprigs sage

A few sprigs thyme

Kosher salt, fresh pepper and chili flakes to taste

Method:

1. *Preheat oven to 375°F and line a sheet pan with parchment paper; set aside.*
2. *Fit Spiralizer with the Wide Ribbon Disc.*
3. *Spiralize the beets then transfer to the sheet pan.*
4. *Sprinkle beets with remaining ingredients.*
5. *Bake for 20-25 minutes or until dry and crispy.*
6. *Remove, garnish as desired and serve warm.*

VEGGIE FRITTATA

Makes 4-5 servings

Ingredients:

2 Russet potatoes, peeled

1 carrot, peeled

1 small red onion

1 zucchini

1 yellow squash

1/2 cup cherry tomatoes, halved

Kosher salt and fresh pepper to taste

8 large eggs

1 1/2 cups cheddar cheese, shredded

Method:

1. *Preheat oven to 400°F.*
2. *Fit Spiralizer with the Julienne Disc.*
3. *Spiralize the potatoes, carrot, onion, zucchini and yellow squash then transfer to a large mixing bowl and add the tomatoes.*
4. *Season with salt and pepper, toss to combine then transfer to a greased 8x8-inch oven-safe dish.*
5. *In a mixing bowl, whisk the eggs, season with salt and pepper then pour over the dish contents.*
6. *Scatter the cheese over the dish contents then bake for 20-25 minutes or until eggs are set and cheese is browned.*
7. *Remove, garnish as desired and serve.*

THAI CHICKEN
SALAD

Makes 4-5 servings

Ingredients:

For the Salad:

2 large carrots

1 daikon radish

1 head iceberg lettuce, chopped

1 bunch green onions, sliced

2 cups leftover chicken, shredded

1 cup jarred peanut sauce

1/2 cup peanuts, chopped

Cilantro sprigs

For Serving:

Soy sauce

Sriracha hot sauce

Lime wedges

Method:

1. *Fit Spiralizer with the Julienne Disc.*
2. *Spiralize the carrots and radish then transfer to a mixing bowl.*
3. *Add the lettuce, green onions and leftover chicken then toss to combine.*
4. *Pour the peanut sauce over the salad and toss to combine.*
5. *Garnish with chopped peanuts and cilantro.*
6. *Serve with soy sauce, sriracha and lime wedges.*

SALT & VINEGAR
POTATO CHIPS

Makes 4 servings

Ingredients:

Canola oil for frying

4 Yukon Gold or Russet potatoes

3 tablespoons white vinegar

Kosher salt to taste

Method:

1. *Preheat oil to 350°F over medium heat using a thermometer.*
2. *Fit Spiralizer with the Narrow Ribbon Disc.*
3. *Spiralize the potatoes, rinse under cold water to remove the surface starch then pat dry using paper towels.*
4. *Sprinkle vinegar evenly over potatoes and let stand for 5 minutes.*
5. *Fry potatoes in batches for 3-5 minutes or until brown and crispy.*
6. *Remove and immediately season with salt before serving hot.*

TIP

If you have a food dehydrator you can use it to make fat-free chips that are delicious. If you love salt and vinegar potato chips as much as I do, purchase powdered vinegar online and sprinkle it over the finished chips. In addition, you can add some salt to a clean coffee grinder to make it into a fine powder that seasons these chips perfectly.

VIETNAMESE QUICK PICKLED CARROTS

Makes 2 servings

Ingredients:

4 large carrots, peeled

1 daikon radish

1/2 cup distilled white vinegar

1/4 cup granulated sugar

1 tablespoon kosher salt

1 cup water

2 tablespoons fresh cilantro, chopped

1 Thai chili pepper

Method:

1. *Fit Spiralizer with the Julienne Disc.*
2. *Spiralize the carrots and daikon radish then transfer to a storage container.*
3. *In a large mixing bowl, whisk together remaining ingredients until the sugar dissolves.*
4. *Pour mixture over the carrots and daikon radish into the storage container.*
5. *Cover and refrigerate for a minimum of 15 minutes before serving.*
6. *These pickled carrots can be kept in the refrigerator for up to 1 week.*

TIP
For a heathier version, you can substitute Stevia sweetener for the sugar in this recipe.

ZOODLE
ZITI

Makes 5-6 servings

Ingredients:

10 large yellow squash

Kosher salt and fresh pepper to taste

1 jar (32 ounces) pasta sauce

1 cup Parmesan cheese, grated

1 package pepperoni, chopped

10 Provolone cheese slices

Method:

1. *Preheat oven to 400°F.*
2. *Fit Spiralizer with the Narrow Ribbon Disc.*
3. *Spiralize the squash then transfer to a large oven-safe baking dish.*
4. *Season squash with salt and pepper.*
5. *In a large mixing bowl, whisk together remaining ingredients, except for Provolone cheese then pour mixture over the squash.*
6. *Place Provolone cheese slices on top of the baking dish contents then bake for 20-25 minutes or until brown and bubbly.*
7. *Remove, garnish as desired and serve.*

MINI SWEET POTATO
PIZZAS

Makes 4 servings

Ingredients:

2 medium sweet potatoes, peeled

2 tablespoons olive oil + more for skillet

Kosher salt and fresh pepper to taste

1 garlic clove, minced

4 tablespoons pasta sauce

Mozzarella cheese, shredded

1/2 red onion, thinly sliced

1/4 cup black olives, sliced

Method:

1. *Fit the Spiralizer with the Julienne Disc.*
2. *Spiralize the sweet potatoes then transfer to a large mixing bowl.*
3. *Add the oil, salt, pepper and garlic to bowl then toss and let stand for 15 minutes to soften.*
4. *Preheat a large skillet over medium-high heat.*
5. *Add a thin film of oil to the skillet.*
6. *Place 4 equal piles of the potato mixture into the skillet then press to form even mounds using a spatula.*
7. *Cook for 4-5 minutes on each side or until golden brown.*
8. *Remove from skillet then top each with pasta sauce, mozzarella, onion and olives.*
9. *Garnish as desired and serve.*

BUTTERNUT SQUASH "PASTA"

Makes 2 servings

Ingredients:

4 yellow squash

2 cups butternut squash, cubed

2 tablespoons olive oil

Kosher salt and fresh pepper to taste

2 garlic cloves, minced

1/4 cup Parmesan cheese, grated

2 tablespoons fresh parsley, chopped

Method:

1. *Fit Spiralizer with the Julienne Disc.*
2. *Spiralize the yellow squash then set aside.*
3. *Preheat a large skillet over medium-high heat then add the butternut squash cubes and oil.*
4. *Season with salt, pepper and garlic then stir for 5 minutes or until brown, tender and hot.*
5. *Add the yellow squash "pasta" to the skillet then toss for 30 seconds to warm it.*
6. *Add the cheese and parsley, toss quickly then divide between 2 bowls and serve immediately.*

VEGGIE RIBBON "NACHOS"

Makes 4 servings

Ingredients:

2 small butternut squash, neck only, peeled

2 tablespoons olive oil

Kosher salt and fresh pepper to taste

1 tablespoon taco seasoning

1 bag (9.6 ounces) precooked hearty sausage crumbles

1 1/2 cups Mexican cheese blend

1 large tomato, diced

1 jalapeño pepper, sliced

1/2 cup black olives, sliced

1 bunch green onions, chopped

Method:

1. *Preheat oven to 400°F and line a sheet pan with parchment paper; set aside.*
2. *Trim butternut squash necks to fit Spiralizer (see tips on page 7).*
3. *Fit Spiralizer with the Narrow Ribbon Disc.*
4. *Spiralize the butternut squash then pile loosely onto the sheet pan.*
5. *Drizzle the squash ribbons with oil then season with salt, pepper and taco seasoning.*
6. *Bake for 10-15 minutes or until dry and edges are beginning to brown.*
7. *Scatter remaining ingredients, except green onions, over the squash ribbons.*
8. *Bake for an additional 10 minutes or until cheese is melted and all ingredients are heated through.*
9. *Remove, top with green onions, garnish as desired and serve.*

TIP

For even crunchier nachos, use the broiler on high for 2-3 minutes instead of baking for 10-15 minutes. This will brown the "nachos" a bit and speed up the process.

PROSCIUTTO SALAD
ROLLS

Makes 2 servings

Ingredients:

1 medium carrot

1 small beet

1 small yellow onion

1 medium zucchini

6 prosciutto slices

2 tablespoons mayonnaise

Kosher salt and fresh pepper to taste

Method:

1. *Fit Spiralizer with the Julienne Disc.*
2. *Spiralize the carrot, beet, onion and zucchini.*
3. *Overlap 3 slices of prosciutto on a cutting board.*
4. *Top evenly with half of the vegetables and 1 tablespoon mayonnaise then season with salt and pepper.*
5. *Gently but firmly roll up into a cylinder.*
6. *Repeat to make a second roll.*
7. *Garnish as desire and serve.*

TERIYAKI CHICKEN "PASTA"

Makes 2 servings

Ingredients:

2 sweet potatoes

3 cups baby spinach

1 garlic clove, minced

1 ginger coin, minced

1/4 cup chicken stock

2 cooked chicken breasts, sliced

1/4 cup bottled Teriyaki sauce

2 green onions, sliced

Soy sauce to taste

Method:

1. *Fit Spiralizer with the Julienne Disc.*
2. *Spiralize the sweet potatoes.*
3. *Divide the spinach between two serving bowls and set aside.*
4. *Preheat a large skillet over medium heat then add the potatoes, garlic, ginger and stock.*
5. *Cook until heated through then divide between the two bowls over the spinach.*
6. *Top with chicken and teriyaki sauce.*
7. *Garnish with green onions and serve with soy sauce.*

GREEN BEAN CASSEROLE

Makes 4-6 servings

Ingredients:

2 medium yellow onions

Oil for frying, such as canola

Kosher salt and fresh pepper to taste

1 cup all purpose flour or cornstarch

1 bag (16 ounces) frozen French cut green beans, thawed

1 can (10 3/4 ounces) cream of mushroom soup

Method:

1. *Fit Spiralizer with the Julienne Disc.*
2. *Spiralize the onions.*
3. *Heat oil for frying to 350°F using a thermometer.*
4. *Season onions with salt and pepper then sprinkle with flour and shake off the excess.*
5. *Fry for 2-3 minutes or until well browned and crispy then remove, drain on paper towels and set aside.*
6. *Preheat oven to 375°F and apply nonstick cooking spray to a baking dish.*
7. *In a mixing bowl, combine the green beans and soup then stir to combine.*
8. *Scrape bean mixture into the prepared dish then bake for 25-30 minutes or until bubbly.*
9. *Remove, top with fried onions, garnish as desired and serve immediately.*

BBQ CARROT CHIPS

Makes 4 servings

Ingredients:

4 large carrots

2 tablespoons vegetable oil

1-2 tablespoons dry BBQ seasoning

Smoked salt and fresh pepper to taste

Method:

1. *Preheat oven to 275°F and line two sheet pans with parchment paper; set aside.*
2. *Fit Spiralizer with the Wide Ribbon Disc.*
3. *Spiralize the carrots then transfer to a large mixing bowl.*
4. *Add remaining ingredients to the mixing bowl then toss gently using your hands.*
5. *Loosely pile carrots onto sheet pans and distribute evenly.*
6. *Bake for 30-45 minutes or until dry, crispy and beginning to brown.*
7. *Carrot chips can be stored in an airtight container at room temperature for up to 1 week.*

TIP
You can change these into taco-flavored chips by sprinkling with some dry taco seasoning.

SKINNY SHRIMP
SCAMPI

Makes 4-5 servings

Ingredients:

2 large zucchini

1 medium sweet potato

1 teaspoon olive oil

1 tablespoon garlic, finely chopped

2 tablespoons onions, finely chopped

1 pound shrimp, peeled and deveined (16-20 per pound)

Kosher salt and fresh pepper to taste

Lemon juice

1/2 cup white wine

Chopped parsley, for serving

Method:

1. *Fit the Spiralizer with the Julienne Disc.*
2. *Spiralize the zucchini and sweet potato.*
3. *Preheat the oil in a large skillet over medium-high heat.*
4. *When oil is hot, add the garlic and onions then cook for 1-2 minutes.*
5. *Add the shrimp, salt, pepper, lemon juice and wine then cook for 3-4 minutes or until shrimp is pink.*
6. *Add the zucchini and sweet potato then toss for 1 minute using tongs.*
7. *Remove, top with parsley, garnish as desired and serve.*

TIP

This recipe is intended to maximize flavor while minimizing calories. If this dish tastes too lean to you, simply drizzle with a tablespoon of melted butter.

VEGGIE ZINGUINI WITH CLAMS

Makes 4-5 servings

Ingredients:

4 zucchini

1 large carrot, peeled

4 tablespoons unsalted butter

1/2 cup canola oil

2 garlic cloves, chopped

2 pounds fresh clams

1 tablespoon fresh basil, chopped

Kosher salt and fresh pepper to taste

Method:

1. *Fit Spiralizer with the Narrow Ribbon Disc.*
2. *Spiralize the zucchini and carrot.*
3. *Preheat a large skillet over medium-high heat then add the butter, oil and garlic.*
4. *Cook until garlic is fragrant then add the clams, basil, salt and pepper.*
5. *Cover with a lid and cook for 4-5 minutes or until clams are open.*
6. *Add the zucchini and carrots to the skillet then toss for 1 minute.*
7. *Remove, garnish as desired and serve.*

SALAD WRAPS

Makes 4 servings

Ingredients:

1 large carrot

6 radishes

1 small beet

2 broccoli stems, peeled if woody (see tips on page 7)

1 firm pear, such as Bosc

4 large raw collard leaves, stems trimmed

1 cup store-bought hummus

Kosher salt and fresh pepper to taste

4 dill pickles, thinly sliced

1/4 cup blue cheese, crumbled

Method:

1. Fit Spiralizer with the Julienne Disc.
2. Spiralize the carrot, radishes, beet, broccoli stems and pear; set aside.
3. Spread each collard leaf with some hummus.
4. Top with the spiralized vegetables and pear, pressing them down into the hummus then season with salt and pepper.
5. Top with pickles and blue cheese then roll up in a burrito-fashion and place seam-side down onto a serving plate.
6. Garnish as desired and serve.

BAKED APPLE
TORNADO

Makes 4 servings

Ingredients:

4 small apples

2 tablespoons unsalted butter, melted

1/4 cup granulated sugar

1/2 teaspoon ground cinnamon

Jarred caramel sauce and whipped cream, for serving

Method:

1. Preheat oven to 350°F and line a sheet pan with parchment paper; set aside.
2. Fit Spiralizer with the Wide Ribbon Disc.
3. Spiralize the apples then transfer to a mixing bowl.
4. Loosely place 4 piles of the apple ribbons onto the sheet pan.
5. Sprinkle ribbons with butter, sugar and cinnamon.
6. Bake for 20-25 minutes or until edges are dry and apples are a pale golden color.
7. Remove and transfer to a serving plate.
8. Garnish with caramel and whipped cream before serving hot.

APPLE CRISPIES

Makes 4 servings

Ingredients:

8 small apples

2 tablespoons granulated sugar

1 teaspoon ground cinnamon

1/2 teaspoon freeze dried vanilla (optional)

Pinch of kosher salt

Method:

1. *Preheat oven to 275°F and line two sheet pans with parchment paper; set aside.*
2. *Fit Spiralizer with the Julienne Disc.*
3. *Spiralize the apples then transfer to a large mixing bowl.*
4. *Sprinkle apples with remaining ingredients then toss gently using your hands.*
5. *Loosely pile apples onto sheet pans and distribute evenly.*
6. *Bake for 30-45 minutes or until dry and beginning to brown.*
7. *Apple crispies can be stored in an airtight container at room temperature for up to 1 week.*

DEVILS ON
HORSEBACK

Makes 12

Ingredients:

1 large zucchini

12 large Medjool dates

1/4 cup stilton or blue cheese

6 bacon slices

12 small bamboo skewers

TIP

For added crunch, tuck a whole almond into the center of the dates along with the blue cheese. You can also use a sliced water chestnut instead of the almonds. In addition, you can wrap carrot strands around the dates for a more colorful presentation.

Method:

1. *Preheat oven to 400°F and line a sheet pan with parchment paper; set aside.*
2. *Fit Spiralizer with the Julienne Disc.*
3. *Spiralize the zucchini then set aside.*
4. *Pit the dates without tearing them in half.*
5. *Place a small amount of cheese where the seed used to be then press to seal in the cheese.*
6. *Cut bacon slices into thirds then wrap each date with a strip of bacon.*
7. *Secure bacon using skewers then repeat using the remaining dates, cheese and bacon.*
8. *Tie strands of zucchini around each date into a bow.*
9. *Place on the sheet pan then bake for 10-15 minutes or until bacon is starting to crisp.*
10. *Remove, garnish as desired and serve.*

HASH BROWNS WITH FRIED EGG

Makes 2 servings

Ingredients:

Yukon gold potatoes, peeled

1 tablespoon olive oil

Kosher salt and fresh pepper to taste

2 large eggs

Method:

1. *Fit Spiralizer with the Julienne Disc.*
2. *Spiralize the potatoes.*
3. *Preheat a large nonstick skillet over medium-high heat.*
4. *Add a thin film of oil to the skillet.*
5. *Place 2 equal piles of the potato mixture into the skillet then press to form even flat portions using a spatula.*
6. *Cook for 4-5 minutes then flip over and cook until both sides are golden brown.*
7. *After flipping the potatoes, move them to one side of the skillet then crack 2 eggs into the other side of the skillet and cook until desired doneness.*
8. *Remove the hash browns from the skillet then top each with a fried egg.*
9. *Garnish as desired and serve.*

PEAR RICOTTA TARTS

Makes 4 tarts

Ingredients:

1 1/2 cups whole milk ricotta cheese

1/2 cup granulated sugar

1/2 teaspoon vanilla extract

4 store-bought tartlette shells

3 firm pears

2 teaspoons fresh lemon juice

1/4 cup powdered sugar

1/4 teaspoon ground cinnamon

Method:

1. *In a mixing bowl, whisk together the ricotta cheese, granulated sugar and vanilla.*
2. *Divide mixture between 4 tartlette shells then set aside.*
3. *Fit Spiralizer with the Julienne Disc.*
4. *Spiralize the pears then transfer to a mixing bowl.*
5. *Add the lemon juice, powdered sugar and cinnamon then stir to coat.*
6. *Divide the pear strands into 4 piles then place on top of ricotta mixture into each shell.*
7. *Garnish as desired and serve immediately.*

TIP

If you would like to make these tarts ahead of time, simply add 1 teaspoon of produce protector such as Fruit-Fresh® powder to the pears to prevent them from darkening. Fruit-Fresh® is found near the gelatin at the grocery store.

PEAR & FARRO SALAD WITH GOAT CHEESE

Makes 4-6 servings

Ingredients:

4 cups farro, cooked and chilled

1/2 cup celery, chopped

1 small radicchio, sliced

1/4 cup chopped pistachio nuts, toasted (see toasting tips on page 7)

1/2 cup store-bought balsamic vinaigrette

1/2 cup black olives, sliced

1/2 cup goat cheese, crumbled

Kosher salt and fresh pepper to taste

2 firm pears

Method:

1. *In a mixing bowl, stir together all ingredients, except pears.*
2. *Fit Spiralizer with the Julienne Disc.*
3. *Spiralize the pears.*
4. *Using scissors, cut pear strands into short lengths then add to the mixing bowl.*
5. *Toss gently to combine, garnish as desired and serve.*

TIP

If you don't have farro, you can substitute it with brown rice or barley.

GREEK SALAD

Makes 4-6 servings

Ingredients:

4 English cucumbers

2 large carrots

1/4 cup extra-virgin olive oil

3 tablespoons red wine vinegar

1 teaspoon honey

2 garlic cloves, minced

2 teaspoons fresh oregano, chopped

Kosher salt and fresh pepper to taste

1 cup Kalamata olives

1/2 cup feta cheese

2 cups grape tomatoes, halved

Method:

1. *Fit Spiralizer with the Wide Ribbon Disc.*
2. *Spiralize the cucumbers and carrots then transfer to a large mixing bowl.*
3. *Add remaining ingredients and toss to coat evenly.*
4. *Garnish as desired and serve.*

TIP

For a vegan salad, substitute maple syrup for the honey and a non-dairy cheese for the feta.

VIETNAMESE BANH MI
SANDWICH

Makes 2 servings

Ingredients:

1 medium carrot

1 small daikon radish

1 teaspoon kosher salt

2 tablespoons rice wine vinegar

1 tablespoon granulated sugar

1 cup leftover chicken

1/4 cup pâté or liverwurst (optional)

2 tablespoons fresh cilantro, chopped

1 jalapeño pepper, sliced

2 pieces French bread

Mayonnaise, for serving

Soy sauce, to taste

TIP
You can make these vegan
by using seasoned tofu,
omitting the pâté and
using vegan mayo.

Method:

1. *Fit Spiralizer with the Julienne Disc.*
2. *Spiralize the carrot and daikon radish then transfer to a mixing bowl.*
3. *Add the salt, vinegar and sugar to the bowl then stir and let stand while assembling the sandwiches.*
4. *Divide the chicken, pâté, carrot-daikon radish mixture, cilantro and jalapeño between the bread pieces.*
5. *Serve with mayonnaise and soy sauce.*

SPINACH, APPLE, BLUE CHEESE SALAD

Makes 4 servings

Ingredients:

2 small apples

1 cup orange juice

1 small red onion

1 bag (6 ounces) baby spinach

1/2 cup pecans, chopped

1/2 cup blue cheese, crumbled

1/2 cup store-bought balsamic dressing

Kosher salt and fresh pepper to taste

Method:

1. *Fit Spiralizer with the Julienne Disc.*
2. *Spiralize apples then immediately place them into a bowl and toss with the orange juice.*
3. *Spiralize the onion then transfer to a separate large mixing bowl.*
4. *Add the spinach, pecans, blue cheese, dressing, salt and pepper to the onions in the mixing bowl then toss to combine.*
5. *Drain the apples and cut into roughly 2-inch pieces using scissors.*
6. *Add apples to the salad, toss again then garnish as desired and serve.*

TIP
You can whisk some of the blue cheese into the vinaigrette to greatly boost the blue cheese taste.

PICKLED RED ONION STRAWS

Makes 4 cups

Ingredients:

4 small red onions

1/2 cup ice water

1/4 cup rice vinegar

1/4 cup granulated sugar

1 tablespoon kosher salt

Method:

1. *Fit Spiralizer with the Julienne Disc.*
2. *Spiralize the onions then transfer to a mixing bowl.*
3. *Add remaining ingredients to the bowl and stir gently.*
4. *Pour into a lidded storage container and serve as desired.*
5. *Onion straws will keep in the refrigerator for up to 1 week.*

TIP

I keep a jar of these in my refrigerator at all times. They add the perfect taste and texture to any salad, sandwich or meat dish.

SUMMER ROLLS

Makes 4 servings

Ingredients:

2 English cucumbers

2 large carrots

8 rice paper wrappers

1/2 pound small shrimp, cooked

16 mint leaves

16 basil leaves

Peanut sauce and crushed peanuts, for dipping

Method:

1. *Fit Spiralizer with the Julienne Disc.*
2. *Spiralize the cucumbers and carrots while keeping them separate from each other.*
3. *Dip one rice paper wrapper in warm water until soft then lay it on a clean flat surface.*
4. *Place some cucumbers, carrots, 3 shrimp, 2 mint leaves and 2 basil leaves on the edge of the rice paper then roll up like a burrito.*
5. *Repeat with remaining ingredients to make additional rolls.*
6. *Garnish as desired and serve with peanut sauce.*

MEXICAN JICAMA
SALAD

Makes 4-6 servings

Ingredients:

3 small jicama

1 small white onion

1 jalapeño pepper, sliced

Zest and juice of 3 limes

2 tablespoons olive oil

Kosher salt and fresh pepper to taste

1/2 teaspoon ground chipotle pepper

Handful of chopped cilantro

Method:

1. *Fit Spiralizer with the Narrow Ribbon Disc.*
2. *Spiralize the jicama and onion then transfer to a mixing bowl.*
3. *Add remaining ingredients and stir gently to combine.*
4. *Garnish as desired and serve.*

MELON FETA SALAD

Makes 5-6 servings

Ingredients:

1 small red onion

Kosher salt and fresh pepper to taste

2 tablespoons extra-virgin olive oil

3 tablespoons fresh lime juice

Handful fresh mint leaves, chopped

3 cups cold honeydew melon, cubed

3 cups cold watermelon, cubed

1/2 cup feta cheese

Method:

1. *Fit the Spiralizer with the Julienne Disc.*
2. *Spiralize the onion.*
3. *In a large bowl, whisk together the salt, pepper, oil, lime juice and mint.*
4. *Add the onions, melons and feta cheese then gently toss to coat.*
5. *Garnish as desired and serve immediately.*

PEAR, GORGONZOLA & WALNUT SALAD

Makes 4 servings

Ingredients:

1 teaspoon fresh lemon zest

4 tablespoons fresh lemon juice

4 tablespoons honey

4 tablespoons walnut or olive oil

Kosher salt and fresh pepper to taste

1 tablespoon fresh parsley, chopped

6 firm pears

1/3 cup gorgonzola or blue cheese, crumbled

1/2 cup toasted walnuts (see toasting tips on page 7)

Method:

1. *In a large mixing bowl, whisk together the lemon zest, juice, honey and oil.*
2. *Add the salt, pepper and parsley then whisk until smooth.*
3. *Fit Spiralizer with the Julienne Disc.*
4. *Spiralize the pears then immediately transfer pears to the mixing bowl.*
5. *Toss pears gently with the dressing to prevent pears from browning.*
6. *Add remaining ingredients and serve immediately.*

MINESTRONE SOUP

Makes 4-6 servings

Ingredients:

1 quart chicken stock

1 cup celery, chopped

1 cup canned kidney beans

1 can (14 ounces) diced tomatoes

6 garlic cloves, chopped

Kosher salt and fresh pepper to taste

3 tablespoons extra-virgin olive oil

4 zucchini

2 large carrots

1 yellow squash

2 small yellow onions

Wedge of Parmesan cheese, for serving

TIP

To make this soup heartier, add 2 cups dry, small shaped pasta such as shells during the last 10 minutes of cooking. You can use whole wheat pasta or even gluten-free pasta if you desire.

Method:

1. In a stockpot over medium-high heat, combine the chicken stock, celery, beans, tomatoes, garlic, salt, pepper and olive oil; let simmer for 20 minutes.
2. Fit Spiralizer with Narrow Ribbon Disc.
3. Spiralize the zucchini, carrots, squash and onions then transfer to the stockpot and simmer for an additional 5 minutes.
4. Pour soup into serving bowls, grate Parmesan cheese on top, garnish as desired and serve.

INDEX

FOR ALL OF MARIAN GETZ'S
COOKBOOKS AS WELL AS
COOKWARE, APPLIANCES, CUTLERY
AND KITCHEN ACCESSORIES
BY WOLFGANG PUCK

PLEASE VISIT
HSN.COM
(KEYWORD: WOLFGANG PUCK)